Oracle Account Receivables

Practice Questions for Interviews and Certification Examination (Release 11i and 12)

Functional Consultant

(150 Questions)

ERP Gold

Printed in the United States of America

First Printing: November 2010

ISBN: 978-1456341954

Oracle Account Receivables Practice Questions for Interviews and Certification Examination

(Release 11i and 12)

Company ABC want to be able to defer all revenue
to an unearned account when they create or import
an invoice, can achieve this?

    A. No, Oracle does not offer such functionality
    B. Yes, by assigning a deferred accounting rule
        to the Invoice
    C. No, they will have to create a custom
        program to do this.
    D. Yes, by assigning invoicing rule to the
        invoice

Question 2 of 150

Which of the following is not a workbench type in
Oracle Account Receivables?

    A. Receipt Workbench.
    B. Transaction Workbench.
    C. Invoice Workbench.
    D. Bills Receivables Workbench.

Question 3 of 150

When you enter receipts individually, Receivables
provides default values for all of the following

attributes in the Receipts and Receipts Summary windows except?

A. Currency
B. Deposit Date
C. GL Date
D. Receipt source

Question 4 of 150

All of the following are profile options that you can set to provide default values in the Receipts Workbench except?

A. AR: Receipt Batch Source to 'Standard'
B. AR: Set Default Receipt Date
C. AR: Default Exchange Rate Type
D. AR: Receipt Batch Source

Question 5 of 150

Which of the following workbench can you use to process your invoices, debit memos, credit memos, on-account credits, charge backs, and adjustments?

A. Invoice Workbench
B. Bill Receivable Workbench
C. Receipts Workbench
D. Transactions Workbench

The system option- Document Number Generation Level determines at what point Receivables generates a document number for transactions, it applies to all of the following except?

    A. Bill Receivables
    B. Adjustment
    C. Chargeback
    D. commitments

You can use the transaction window to enter all of the following transactions except?

    A. Bill Receivables
    B. Invoices
    C. Debit Memo
    D. Commitments

When you enter an invoice, Receivables uses which of the following to determine your default general ledger accounts?

    A. AutoAccounting

B. AutoInvoicing
C. Financial Option
D. Account Generator

Question 9 of 150

You can view the detail accounting lines for existing transactions in Account Receivables in the form of a balanced accounting entry (i.e., debits equal credits) using?

A. The Sub Ledger Accounting Module
B. The View Accounting Window
C. The Trial Balance Report
D. The Review Transaction Details Window

Question 10 of 150

You can assign revenue and non-revenue sales credits for all of the following except?

A. Invoices
B. Credit memos
C. Commitments
D. Debit memos

Question 11 of 150

For rule-based transactions, you cannot use which of the following workbench to update sales credits or modify salespeople after Revenue Recognition has run, even if the transaction is incomplete?

A. Transaction Workbench
B. Invoice Workbench
C. Bill Receivable Workbench
D. Receipt Workbench

Question 12 of 150

When updating sales credits in the Transactions workbench, you must not rerun Auto Accounting if all of the following are true except?

A. Auto Accounting is based on salesperson.
B. The AR: Allow Update of Existing Sales Credits profile option is set to Yes
C. You have previously adjusted revenue on this transaction using the RAM wizard.
D. If AutoAccounting is based on sales credits.
E. None of the above

Question 13 of 150

To safely update sales credits on transactions whose revenue was already adjusted, you should always use?

- A. AutoAccounting
- B. AutoInvoice
- C. RAM wizard
- D. Concurrent program

Question 14 of 150

Which of the following let you determine when to recognize the receivable for invoices that span more than one accounting period?
- A. Revenue Recognition
- B. Invoice Rule
- C. Auto Accounting Rule
- D. Accounting Rule

Question 15 of 150

Company ABC wants their Oracle Receivables to be able to automatically create the payment schedules based on the invoice date and the payment terms that they define, Oracle can do this using?

A. Descriptive flex field
B. Split payment term functionality
C. Create installment functionality
D. Auto Invoice functionality

Question 16 of 150

If Company ABC requires the precise recognition of revenue for a schedule that includes both full and partial accounting periods, then you can use an accounting rule of?

A. Daily revenue rate, total Periods
B. Daily revenue rate, partial periods
C. Daily revenue rate, full periods
D. Daily revenue rate, monthly periods

Question 17 of 150

Which of the following is used to create revenue and offset accounting distributions for individual invoice lines with accounting rules and also enable you to split revenue for a line over one or more revenue or offset accounts?

A. Accounting rules

B. Accounting Sets
C. Invoice rule
D. Invoice sets

Question 18 of 150

Which of the following program identifies all new transactions and creates the revenue distributions for those transactions?

A. Recurring Invoice Program
B. Master program
C. Revenue Recognition Program
D. AutoInvoice Master program

Question 19 of 150

When importing invoices, AutoInvoice determines the invoice GL date and the transaction date using which of the following method:

A. If you use Bill in Advance as the invoicing rule, AutoInvoice uses the earliest start date of the accounting rules associated with your invoice lines as the GL date of the invoice.
B. If you use Bill in Arrears as the invoicing rule and the invoice line have a Fixed Schedule accounting rule and a period of Specific Date, AutoInvoice sets the GL date

and transaction dates equal to the latest Specific Date of the accounting rule.
C. For all other accounting rules using the Bill in Arrears invoicing rule, AutoInvoice first computes an ending date for each invoice line based on the accounting rule, accounting rule start date, and duration. AutoInvoice then uses the latest specific date for both the invoice GL date and the transaction date.
D. All of the above

Question 20 of 150

You can still adjust the exchange rate of a foreign currency transaction once it has been posted or has had a receipt applied to it?

True
False

Question 21 of 150

You can adjust the account assignments of invoices that you wish to credit in all of the following ways except?

A. LIFO
B. FIFO

C. Prorate
D. Unit

Question 22 of 150

Receivables let you create the following types of commitments?

    A. Deposit and charge backs
    B. Guarantees and Contractual Agreements
    C. Deposit and Guarantees
    D. Charge Backs and Contractual Agreements

Question 23 of 150

A batch has a status that indicates whether it is complete. A batch can have all of the following statuses except?

    A. Pending
    B. Closed
    C. New
    D. Out of Balance

You can void a transaction in Oracle Receivables if?

  A. It does not have any activity against it.
  B. It has not been processed by the Revenue
     Recognition program.
  C. It has not been posted to your general
     ledger.
  D. All of the above.
  E. None of the above

When you copy invoices, Receivables derive the
exchange rates and tax rates from?

  A. The copied invoice date
  B. The copied invoice Account Information
  C. The date of your first copied invoice
  D. From E-business Tax Application

Company ABC wants Oracle Receivable to be able
to recognize the exact amount of revenue for
multiple periods in a schedule at a very granular
level, which of the following oracle functionality
can they use to achieve the above?

A. Invoice rule
B. Auto accounting rule
C. Accounting rule
D. Revenue recognition

Question 27 of 150

All of the following are adjustment statuses in Receivables except?

A. Approved
B. Research- Required
C. Rejected
D. Concluded

Question 28 of 150

All of the following are XML receivables documents types except?

A. Invoices
B. Debit memos
C. Credit memos
D. Adjustments

Question 29 of 150

You can import transactions into Oracle Receivables using?

    A. Oracle Interface Table program
    B. Auto Invoice program
    C. Auto Accounting program
    D. Application Desktop Integrator program

Question 30 of 150

Which of the following is not true about credit transactions in Receivables?

    A. Receivables let you credit an entire invoice or specific invoice lines.
    B. When you credit a transaction, Receivables creates the appropriate accounting entries and debit any sales credit assigned to your salespeople.
    C. Use the Credit Transactions window to enter, update, and review credit memos against specific invoices, debit memos, or commitments.
    D. You can also credit freight for an entire invoice or only for specific invoice lines.

In Receivables, transactions with no activity against them can be removed by which of the following methods?

A. Delete the invoice in the Transactions window by choosing Delete Record from the Edit menu.
B. Void the invoice by changing the invoice's type in the Transaction window to a type with Open Receivables and Post to GL options set to No.
C. Reverse the distributions by creating a Credit Memo against the invoice
D. All of the above

Question 32 of 150

To cancel a submission of the Auto Invoice Master program, you must cancel each child program individually and not the master program itself

A. True
B. False

Question 33 of 150

An accounting period can have all of the following

statuses in Receivables except

A. Closed
B. Closed pending
C. Open
D. Not closed

Question 34 of 150

Receivables use which of the following information to convert your foreign currency receipt and transaction amounts to your functional currency?

A. Multi-currency
B. Exchange Rates
C. Translation
D. Currency Rates

Question 35 of 150

If you are crediting a transaction that has multiple installments, Receivables allows you to choose which of the following Split Term Method(s)?

A. LIFO
B. Prorates
C. FIFO
D. All of the above
E. None of the above

If you are reviewing a credit memo against a
specific invoice or commitment, Receivables
derives the default sales credits from?

A. The original invoice
B. Commitment sales credit line
C. From the credit memo
D. Both A and B
E. Both B and C

You can apply the on-account credit memo to one
or more open debit items to either reduce or close
the on-account credit memo and your customer's
outstanding balance.

A. True
B. False

Receivables let you fully or partially credit your
invoices while it automatically creates all the
accounting reversal entries for you. You can use
which of the following window to create credit
memos?

A. Credit invoice window
B. Auto Invoice
C. Auto Accounting
D. None of the above

Question 39 of 150

Which of the following program is used to transfer transactions from other systems into Receivables?

A. Auto Invoice program
B. Auto Invoice Import program
C. Auto Import program
D. Auto invoice transfer program

Question 40 of 150

You can create _____ on your Transaction Flexfield columns if you want to query transaction flexfield information in your invoice headers and line.

A. Structures
B. Indexes
C. Segment qualifiers
D. Lines

All of the following are types of transaction flexfields except?

   A. Link-To Transaction Flexfield
   B. Index Transaction Flexfield
   C. Invoice Transaction Flexfield
   D. Reference Transaction Flexfield

Receivables provide the following commitment transaction types?

   A. Deposits and Guarantees
   B. Budgets and Deposits
   C. Guarantees and Budget
   D. None of the above

Revenue Recognition will create the distribution records for an unearned revenue account, if which of the following rules exist?

   A. Auto Accounting rules
   B. Invoice rules
   C. Accounting rules

D. Deferred accounting rules

Question 44 of 150

Which of the following integrates with Receivables to ensure that, during revenue recognition and deferral activities in Receivables, COGS (Cost of Goods Sold) is recognized or deferred in the same percentage as revenue?

A. Oracle Inventory
B. Oracle Sales management
C. Oracle costing
D. All of the above

Question 45 of 150

Receivables automatically create which of the following report whenever you run the Revenue Recognition program, the Revenue Recognition Master program, or the Submit Accounting program.

A. Revenue recognition execution report
B. Revenue recognition report
C. Revenue recognition detail report
D. All of the above

You must assign your reporting set of books to your primary set of books if you are using which of the following functionalities?

A. Auto Accounting
B. Multiple Reporting Currencies
C. Auto Invoice
D. Territory Flexfield

Question 47 of 150

When you create an adjustment that is outside of your approval limits, Receivables creates an adjustment with a status of?

A. Pending
B. Research- Required
C. Rejected
D. Concluded

Question 48 of 150

You can make sales credit adjustments to which of the following?

A. Completed Invoice
B. Debit Memos
C. Credit memo
D. All of the above

Question 49 of 150

To make revenue adjustments to on account credit memos you must?

A. Set the profile option AR: Use invoice accounting for credits profile option to No
B. The invoicing rule must be In Advance
C. The Accounting rule must be In Advance
D. Set the profile option AR: Use invoice accounting for credits profile option to Yes

Question 50 of 150

When you make adjustments using Revenue Accounting, Receivables uses _____ to automatically generate all necessary accounting distributions.

A. Auto Invoice
B. Auto Invoice program
C. Auto Accounting
D. Auto Distribution Program

Question 51 of 150

System administrator can use _____ to prevent users with your responsibility from performing specific Receivables operations?

    A. Responsibility Security
    B. Menu Security
    C. Form Security
    D. Function Security

Question 52 of 150

When you query a transaction, the Revenue Accounting and Sales Credits window displays which of the following information?

    A. The Transaction tab displays transaction details, including a summary of the scheduled and unscheduled revenue on the transaction.
    B. Revenue is scheduled when Receivables creates, for a transaction line, the revenue distribution records for all accounting periods as specified by the line's assigned accounting rule.
    C. The Actions History tab displays details about actions already recorded against this transaction.
    D. All of the above

Question 53 of 150

You can use the Revenue Accounting Management (RAM) wizard to?

    A. Adjust revenue
    B. Record Sales credits
    C. Record early customer acceptance
    D. Manage revenue contingencies

Question 54 of 150

When applying cross currency receipts, your customer needs to provide you with which of the following remittance information?

    A. To which invoice(s) this receipt should be applied.
    B. If the receipt is a partial payment, how much of each invoice is to be settled (this is the 'Amount Applied' field in the Applications window).
    C. How much of the receipt should be allocated to this transaction (this is the 'Allocated Receipt Amount' field in the Applications window),
    D. All of the above

Question 55 of 150

This report lets you analyze each cross currency receipt application for a customer, customer site, and receipt date range and receipt currency?

    A. Cross Currency Detail report
    B. Cross Currency Exchange Gain/Loss report
    C. Calculate gain and loss report
    D. Receivables receipt details report.

Question 56 of 150

A realized gain or loss occurs when the exchange rate changes between the invoice date and the receipt date?

    A. True
    B. False

Question 57 of 150

Which of the following determine the steps Receivables uses to apply partial payments and credit memos to your customer's open debit items, and how discounts affect the open balance for each type of associated charges?

    A. Accounting rule sets
    B. AutoAccounting rule sets

C. Application Rule Sets

D. Invoicing rule sets

Question 58 of 150

Before your company can transfer and receive XML messages with a customer, you and your customer must agree to and implement the following except?

A. Oracle Report Manager (ORM) or your customer can implement a program that understands the ORM protocol.

B. OAG standard and version 7.2.1 of the DTDs

C. Invoice information defined in the user area section of the XML DTDs.

D. Unique trading partner identifier, such as the Source Trading Partner Location code in XML Gateway

Question 59 of 150

Company ABC want to be able to automates the timing of revenue recognition for manually entered invoices, or invoices imported via Auto Invoice, how can they achieve this?

A. Oracle can automates the timing of revenue recognition for invoices imported via Auto

Invoice but not manually entered invoices.
B. By using the Revenue Management Engine
C. By Using the Revenue Recognition Program
D. Oracle cannot do this

Question 60 of 150

When importing invoices, AutoInvoice determines the accounting rule start dates using which of the following method?

A. If your invoice has an accounting rule with a type Fixed Schedule and a period of Specific Date, AutoInvoice uses the earliest accounting rule date as your rule start date.
B. If you elected to derive the rule start date, AutoInvoice first uses the ship date in the interface table. If the ship date does not exist, AutoInvoice uses the sales order date. If the sales order date does not exist, AutoInvoice uses the date you entered in the Run AutoInvoice window.
C. If your invoice does not use a Fixed Schedule accounting rule with a specific date period, or you have not elected to derive the rule start date, then AutoInvoice uses the default date you specified in the Run AutoInvoice window.
D. All of the above
E. None of the above

Which of the following ensures that the columns in Receivables' Interface tables reference the appropriate values and columns in Receivables?

    A. Auto Accounting validation program
    B. AR interface table validation program
    C. Auto Invoice validation program
    D. AR-Interface validation program

Company ABC does not want to recognize revenue until payment is received for certain revenue contingencies that places the likelihood of collectibility in doubt, how can they achieve this in Oracle receivables?

    A. Manually enter payment when received and oracle will recognize revenue afterwards.
    B. Oracle Receivables automates this process with Payment-Based Revenue Management.
    C. Oracle Receivables automates this process with Oracle Payables
    D. Oracle does not offer such capability.

Question 63 of 150

Which of the following is used to uniquely identify each transaction and transaction line you import through Auto Invoice?

A. Transaction Flex field
B. Auto Accounting Program
C. Territory Flex field
D. Auto Invoice Program

Question 64 of 150

You can create which of the following with a structure similar to the Line Transaction Flexfield, but only include header level segments. For example, if the Line Transaction Flexfield structure has four segments and the last two segments contain line level information, you define it using the first two segments only?

A. Link-To Transaction Flexfield
B. Index Transaction Flexfield
C. Invoice Transaction Flexfield
D. Reference Transaction Flexfield

The Revenue Management Engine initially defers revenue on the sum of all line balances, excluding which of the following?

    A. Taxes
    B. Freight
    C. Late charges
    D. All of the above
    E. None of the above

Payment-based revenue management occurs when deferred revenue exists on the invoice due to which of the following revenue contingencies?

    A. Creditworthiness
    B. Extended Payment Term
    C. Doubtful Collectibility
    D. All of the above

Deferred revenue can exist on an invoice due to a combination of the contingencies listed below except?

    A. Creditworthiness

B. Doubtful Collectibility
C. time-based
D. Applied Payment

Question 68 of 150

You can enter which of the following types of receipts in Receivables?

A. Standard receipts and miscellaneous receipts
B. Blanket receipts and miscellaneous receipts
C. Standard receipts and Blanket receipts
D. None of the above

Question 69 of 150

A receipt can have all of the following statuses except?

A. Approved
B. Pending
C. Confirmed
D. Reversed

Receivables provides all of the following invoicing rule(s) except?

A. Bill in Advances
B. Bill in Arrears
C. Bill Later
D. All of the above

You can use all of the following rules to copy an invoice except?

A. Annual
B. Quarterly
C. Multiple copy
D. Single copy

You can either pass your accounts through the AutoInvoice Interface tables or have AutoAccounting determine them and can even pass some of your accounts and have AutoAccounting determine the rest.

A. True
B. False

You can apply receipts to any type of transaction except?

    A. Guarantees and standard credit memos
    B. Deposits and Debit Memos
    C. Guarantees and Deposits
    D. Credit memos and Debit memos

Which of the following refer to the number of days after the discount term that your customer can take earned discounts?

    A. Grace days
    B. Discounted days
    C. Earned Discount days
    D. None of the above

If you set up Receivables to use_____, you can apply a receipt in one currency to one or more transactions in different currencies.

    A. Cross currency receipts
    B. Multi Currency
    C. Foreign Currency

D. Multi Currency receipt

Question 76 of 150

Before you can use the Revenue Accounting
Management (RAM) wizard you must perform
which of the following prerequisite(s)?

A. Set profile option
B. Create Revenue Adjustment Reason
Lookup Codes
C. Recognize Revenue
D. All of the above

Question 77 of 150

Open receipts include receipts that have?

A. Unapplied cash
B. On-account cash
C. Open claim investigation applications
D. All of the above

Question 78 of 150

When netting receipts, both receipts must be in the
same?

A. Currency
B. Set of Book
C. Operating unit
D. Organization

Question 79 of 150

Your customers can use any of these Oracle Payments, payment methods to make a prepayment except?

A. Cash
B. Automatic Clearing House (ACH) bank account transfer
C. Money orders
D. Direct debit

Question 80 of 150

As with same currency receipt applications, Receivables accounts for your FXGL using the Realized Gains and Realized Losses accounts that you defined in the?

A. Transaction window
B. Receipt window
C. System Options window
D. Foreign Currency window

Which of the following is true about adjustment?

A. Create adjustments to increase or decrease the balance due for an invoice, debit memo, chargeback, or commitment.
B. You can create an adjustment to write off the remaining amount and close the debit item.
C. If you create an adjustment during a receipt application (for example, to write off a small remaining amount) and then unapply the application later, Receivables reverses the adjustment and assigns it a status of 'Adjustment Reversal.'
D. All of the above.

Question 82 of 150

Non-invoice related transactions such as investment and interest income are known as _____ in Receivables?

A. Miscellaneous receipts
B. Non Invoice receipt
C. Non-related receipts
D. Non-Invoice transactions

Question 83 of 150

You can reverse which of the following type(s) of receipts?

    A. Invoice-related receipts
    B. Non-invoice related (miscellaneous) receipts
    C. Credit Card refund (negative miscellaneous) receipts
    D. All of the above

Question 84 of 150

Receivables lets you create two types of receipt reversals, these are?

    A. Standard Reversal and Automatic Reversal
    B. Debit Memo Reversal and Credit Memo Reversal
    C. Standard Reversal and Debit Memo Reversal
    D. Automatic Reversal and Credit Memo Reversal

Question 85 of 150

You can reapply which of the following types of receipts?

A. Automatic and manually entered receipts
B. Standard and Automatic receipts
C. Debit memo receipt and Credit memo Receipts
D. Automatic and standard receipts

Question 86 of 150

Use the Notes Receivable reports to review note statuses. A note can have all of the following statuses except?

A. Confirmed
B. Approved
C. Matures
D. Delinquent

Question 87 of 150

You can select up to _____ credit classifications that indicate noncredit worthiness in the Revenue Policy page?

A. Two
B. Four
C. Three
D. Five

When you create a cross currency receipt application, the resulting accounting entry includes which of the following?

    A. Accounting currency
    B. Receipt currency
    C. Functional currency
    D. All of the above

All of the following are valid note activities in Receivables except?

    A. Deposit
    B. Guaranteed
    C. Exchange
    D. Factor

Which of the following is not true about applying receipts?

    A. You can apply receipts to any type of transaction except guarantees and deposits.
    B. You can apply all or part of a receipt or on-

account credit to a single debit item or to several debit items.

C. You can apply receipts to an entire transaction and prorate the receipt amount across all transaction lines.

D. You can apply a receipt to an unrelated customer's debit items if the system option Allow Payment of Unrelated Invoices is set to Yes.

Which of the following is true about the Revenue Management Engine?

A. It considers any existing revenue contingencies when evaluating your invoices for revenue recognition.

B. If an invoice has one or more contingencies, then the Revenue Management Engine immediately post revenue.

C. The Revenue Management Engine does not analyze collectibility for invoices that are assigned deferred accounting rules.

D. If an invoice has no contingency, then the Revenue Management Engine immediately recognizes revenue (for invoices without rules) or recognizes revenue according to the initially assigned accounting rules (for invoices with rules).

Question 92 of 150

You must create a debit memo reversal if?

A. You are reversing a receipt with a remitted credit card refund application.
B. You are reversing a receipt (Receipt A) that was applied to another receipt (Receipt B), if the reversal would draw Receipt B's balance negative.
C. You are reversing a receipt from which you have created a chargeback and this chargeback has had activity against it (for example, another receipt, credit memo, or adjustment).
D. All of the above

Question 93of 150

All of the following steps must be completed in the order to set up your system to create notes receivable except?

A. Define Banks and Bank Accounts
B. Define Auto Accounting
C. Define Receipt Classes
D. Assign Receipt Methods and Remittance Banks

Which of the following is a service that commercial banks offer corporate customers to enable them to outsource their accounts receivable payment processing?

    A. AutoLockbox (or Lockbox)
    B. AutoPayment
    C. Customer payment processing center
    D. Note Receivables

In order to use the AutoAssociate functionality you must?

    A. Check the AutoAssociate box when defining your Lockbox (Lockboxes window).
    B. Ensure that all invoices to which any single receipt will be applied belong to the same customer.
    C. Ensure that the matching numbers within your transmission are unique.
    D. All of the above

Which of the following is not true about
AutoLockbox?

A. The AutoLockbox validation program will
   identify a customer for a receipt using the
   matching number only if all of the
   transactions listed to be paid by this receipt
   are associated with the same customer.
B. If a unique customer cannot be determined,
   AutoLockbox imports the receipt and
   assigns it a status of Unidentified.
C. If a unique customer cannot be determined
   and duplicate invoices are supplied as the
   matching number for a receipt,
   AutoLockbox does not validate the receipt
   because it cannot determine how to apply
   the receipt
D. All of the above are true.

Question 97 of 150

To use AutoCash rules to apply receipts imported
using Lockbox, you must?

A. Include the MICR or customer number in
   your transmission.
B. Do not include matching numbers in your
   transmission (otherwise, Post QuickCash
   will apply the receipt to each transaction for

which it can find a match).
C. Specify an AutoCash Rule set for your customer's profile class (otherwise, Receivables uses the AutoCash Rule set in the System Options window).
D. All of the above are true.

Question 98of 150

When you enter receipts in the QuickCash window or import them using AutoLockbox, Receivables stores them in the?

A. Interface Tables
B. Database
C. Interim tables
D. Staging Tables

Question 99 of 150

Following are the AutoCash rules you can use except?

A. Match Payment with Invoice
B. Clear the Account
C. Clear Past Due Invoices
D. Post Past Due Invoices Grouped by Payment Term.

Question 100 of 150

Receivables lets you use the following types of discounts except?

    A. Earned and Unearned Discounts
    B. Offset Discounts
    C. Discounts on Partial Payments
    D. Tiered Discounts

Question 101 of 150

You can write off the receipt if?

    A. If you leave partial receipt amounts unapplied.
    B. If a receipt underpays an invoice.
    C. If the receipt is imported from a third party application
    D. Both B and C
    E. Both A and B
    F. None of the above

Question 102 of 150

In order to create Manual Receipt Write-Offs all of the following must be in place except?

    A. Define your system level write-off limits for

receipts
B. Define AutoLock box
C. Define Receipt Write-off approval limits.
D. Define receivable activities using the Receipt Write-off activity type.

Question 103 of 150

In order to use the Payables and Receivables Netting feature in Oracle Receivables you must?

A. You must set up a paying relationship for the customers.
B. Associate the bank account used in the netting agreement with the AP/AR Netting receipt class.
C. Enable the Allow Payment of Unrelated Transactions Receivables System Option.
D. All of the above are true.

Question 104 of 150

To let your customers pay by ACH bank account transfer, you must perform all of the following except?

A. Define a receipt method with a payment method of Bank Account Transfer.

B. Assign this receipt method to an automatic receipt class.
C. Enter bank information for the ACH depositing bank and assign the receipt method and payment instrument to the transaction (in the Payment Details region of the Transactions window)
D. Set the ACH Bank Account profile option to 'Always used' or 'Partially used.

Question 105 of 150

If automatic customer numbering is set to No, when you enter a new customer, you must enter the all of the following except?

A. Customer's name
B. Customer's Address
C. Customer's profile class
D. Customer's number

Question 106 of 150

All of the following are types of aging bucket except?

A. 4- Bucket Aging
B. 7- Bucket Aging
C. 5- Bucket Aging

D. Credit Snapshot

Question 107 of 150

All of the following are application rules type in Receivables except?

    A. Line First - Tax After
    B. Prorate All
    C. Prorate None
    D. Line and Tax Prorate

Question 108 of 150

All of the following are optional set up steps during Oracle Receivable configuration except?

    A. Define Units of Measure
    B. Define Standard Memo Lines
    C. Set Up Cross Currency Receipts
    D. Define Unit of Measure Classes

AutoLockbox completes all of the following validations except?

    A. Lockbox Level Validation
    B. Batch Level Validation
    C. Account Level
    D. Line Level Validation

Creating automatic receipts involves all of the following steps except?

    A. Create: Select the invoices to include in your automatic receipts.
    B. Approve: Update, delete, and approve the receipts that you have selected.
    C. Post: Post your receipts
    D. Format: Format your automatic receipts onto paper to send to your customer for confirmation or notification before remitting them to your bank on either paper or magnetic media.

Receivables support which of the following types of remittances?

    A. Standard and Automatic
    B. Factored and Miscellaneous
    C. Standard and Factored
    D. Miscellaneous and Automatic

You must complete which of these steps to process credit card payments in Receivables?

    A. Assign a credit card receipt method and credit card payment instrument to the transactions that you want to pay by credit card.
    B. Run the Automatic Receipts program to select the transactions that are flagged for credit card payment.
    C. Approve the batch of automatic receipts to reserve the payment amount from your cardholder's account and close the selected transactions.
    D. None of the above
    E. All of the above are true.

You can create credit card transactions in
Receivables by?

   A. Manually creating them in the Transactions
      window
   B. Importing them using AutoInvoice
   C. Both A and B
   D. Manually creating them in the Receipts
      window

AutoInvoice will reject a credit memo from
automated receipt handling if which of the
following conditions exists on the transaction to be
credited?

   A. The original invoice's transaction type is set
      to allow over application
   B. An on-account credit memo was already
      applied against the invoice.
   C. An adjustment already exists against the
      invoice:
   D. All of the above
   E. None of the above

Question 115 of 150

AutoInvoice might automatically place on account the amount of a refund request, if:

A. Installments exist and are not fully paid.
B. Receipt chargeback (noninvoice-related)
C. Multiple payment types (ACH, cash, credit card) exist on the same transaction to be credited.
D. The amount of the refund request is less than the minimum refund amount specified in your system options.
E. All of the above

Question 116 of 150

There are four methods in Oracle Receivables for exchanging transactions for bills receivable except?

A. Automatically, by submitting the Bills Receivable Batch Creation concurrent program in the Submit Request window
B. Manually by creating a bills receivable batch using the Bills Receivable Transaction Batches window
C. Directly, by exchanging a transaction in the Transactions window for a bill receivable
D. Manually, using the Bills Receivable window and the Assignments window

Question 117 of 150

If only one transaction is exchanged for a bill receivable, then Receivables uses the transaction number as the bill number if?

A. The Inherit Transaction Number box is checked for the bills receivable creation receipt method assigned to the exchanged transaction.
B. The transaction number is not already used by another transaction with the same batch source as the bill receivable.
C. All of the above
D. None of the above

Question 118 of 150

AutoLockbox is a three step process that involves all of the following except?

A. Import
B. Export
C. Validation
D. Post QuickCash

A bills receivable batch has all of the following statuses after it is submitted except?

A. Creation Started
B. Creation Completed
C. Creation Stopped
D. Draft

You can print bills receivable in all of the following ways except?

A. Individually
B. Bills Receivable Batch
C. Bill Receivable Remittance Batch
D. All of the above

Receivables use which of the following tables to store your chargeback information?

A. RA_CUST_TRX_LINE_GL_DIST
B. AR_ADJUSTMENTS
C. AR_PAYMENT_SCHEDULES
D. All of the above

E. None of the above

Question 122 of 150

All of the following are receivable reports except?

    A. Bills Receivable By Status report
    B. Automatic Transactions Batch report
    C. Bill Receivables Detail report
    D. Bills Receivable Stamp Values

Question 123 of 150

The Customers set of pages comes with Oracle Trading Community Architecture (TCA) Data Quality Management (DQM) feature, the DQM feature lets you?

    A. Perform advanced searches for parties and customer accounts with user-defined criteria.
    B. Prevent duplicate entries by determining if the customer that you are creating or updating is a potential duplicate of any existing customer.
    C. Prevent duplicate transactions from posting within Oracle Receivables.
    D. Both A and B
    E. Both B and C

Question 124 of 150

The relationship type that you use to create a party paying relationship must meet which of the following requirements?

   A. The relationship type must be hierarchical, and the subject and object parties must be of type Organization.
   B. The relationship type must be assigned to one of these relationship groups, either: a Pay Within group or Pay Below.
   C. All of the above
   D. None of the above

Question 125 of 150

Before the integration with Advanced Collections was available, Receivables offered which of the following dunning methods?

   A. Automatic Dunning
   B. Staged Dunning
   C. Days Overdue:
   D. Both A and B
   E. Both B and C

Question 126 of 150

When a customer is consistently late in making payments, has exceeded their credit limit, or is identified as a bad risk, you can prevent additional credit purchases by placing their account on

    A. Credit stop
    B. Debit stop
    C. Credit hold
    D. Debit hold
    E. Credit check

Question 127 of 150

From the Late Charges Batches window, you can do which of the following?

    A. View batches of draft or final late charges
    B. Delete draft late charge batches
    C. Submit your modified batch for final late charge calculation.
    D. All of the above

Question 128 of 150

Receivables let you define credit profiles for each customer and each of their bill-to locations using the Customer Profile Classes window. Profile classes let you choose whether to send statements to customers using this profile class and, if so, let you specify?

A. A statement cycle
B. A minimum statement amount by currency
C. Whether to send a statement to customers if they have a credit balance.
D. All of the above

Question 129 of 150

You can choose one of the following options as your discount basis in Oracle Receivables except?

A. Invoice Amount
B. Lines, Freight Items and Tax
C. Lines and Tax, not Freight Items and Tax
D. All of the above are true.

Question 130 of 150

You can mark manually entered transactions for credit card payment by specifying which of the following information?

A. Paying customer information

B. The receipt method that you defined for your credit card transactions
C. The Oracle Payments payment instrument
D. All of the above

Question 131 of 150

Lockbox only uses MICR numbers to associate a customer with a receipt if which of the following is true?

A. The customer number is not included in the transmission.
B. The MICR number is included in the transmission.
C. Both A and B
D. None of the above

Question 132 of 150

AutoLockbox checks all of the following locations for the Match Receipts By parameter except?

A. Customer Bill-to Site
B. Customer
C. Customer Address
D. Lockbox

All of the following are true about open and close period except?

    A. Open and close accounting periods in your calendar to control the recording of accounting information for these periods

    B. Receivables lets you open future accounting periods while your current period is still open.

    C. Receivables will not let you reopen previously closed accounting periods.

    D. Receivables let you enter receivables activities without transferring transactions to the general ledger when you set the accounting periods to 'Future.'

    E. All of the above are true.

Question 134 of 150

Which of the following determine the number of periods and percentage of total revenue to record in each accounting period?

    A. Revenue Recognition

    B. Invoice Rule

    C. Auto Accounting Rule

    D. Accounting Rule

Question 135 of 150

Which of the following is not true about accounting in Receivables?

A. Store a complete and balanced subledger journal entry in a common data model for each business event that requires accounting.
B. Maintain multiple accounting representations for a single business event, resolving conflicts between corporate and local fiscal accounting requirements
C. Retain the most granular level of detail in the subledger, with different summarization options in the general ledger, allowing full auditability and reconciliation because the link between transaction and accounting data is preserved.
D. All of the above
E. Both B and C

Question 136 of 150

The accounting event entities for Receivables are all of the following except?

A. Transactions
B. Commitments
C. Bills Receivable

D. Adjustments

Question 137 of 150

When you run AutoAccounting, Receivables?

A. Assigns valid Accounting Flexfields to your invoices and credit memos
B. Automatically generates valid Accounting Flexfields for your Freight, Receivable, Revenue, AutoInvoice Clearing, Tax, Unbilled Receivable, and Unearned Revenue Accounts.
C. Controls how your Accounting Flexfields are created and defined
D. Does all of the above

Question 138 of 150

Receivables automatically create default Accounting Flexfields for each invoice and credit memo for your?

A. Revenue
B. Freight
C. Receivable
D. Tax accounts
E. All of the above

Question 139 of 150

Oracle Subledger Accounting provides all of the following accounting reports that you can run from an Oracle Receivables responsibility to review accounting information except?

    A. Account Analysis report
    B. Third Party Balances report
    C. Closed Account Balances Listing (its open)
    D. Multi period Accounting reports

Question 140 of 150

Which of the following is a reconciliation method in Receivables?

    A. External and Internal
    B. Internal and Subledger Accounting
    C. Subledger Accounting and GL
    D. None of the above

Question 141 of 150

Which of the following is not true about accrual accounting in Receivables?

    A. Creation of transactions such as invoices, debit memos, deposits and chargebacks

affect the account balances immediately.
B. Accounting Rules are redundant as revenue will be recognized only when payment is received.
C. Receipts can be reversed using the Standard Reversal or Debit memo reversal.
D. Deposits and Guarantees both affect on-account balances in Receivables.

Question 142of 150
You must be aware of which of the following when creating transaction types to be used with Cash Basis Accounting?

A. If you set 'Open Receivable' to No, the transactions will never be posted.
B. Cash Basis method of accounting does not permit you to set 'Open Receivable' to Yes and 'Post To GL' to No.
C. Creation Signs must be either positive or negative for all transactions. They cannot be of type 'Any Sign'.
D. All of the above
E. None of the above

Question 143 of 150

Receivables use which of the following tables to store your receipt information?

A. AR_CASH_RECEIPTS
B. AR_CASH_RECEIPT_HISTORY
C. AR_PAYMENT_SCHEDULES
D. All of the above
E. None of the above

Question 144 of 150

The Post QuickCash program uses which of the following rules to determine how to automatically apply your receipts?

A. AutoAccounting rules
B. AutoCash rules
C. Accounting rules
D. Invoicing rules

Question 145 of 150

Which of the following report parameter(s) is common to many Receivables reports?

A. Adjust Amount in Foreign Currency
B. Approval Limits
C. Balance Due
D. All of the above
E. None of the above

Question 146 of 150

All of the following are reconciliation report types in Receivables except?

    A. Aging 7-Buckets - By Account
    B. Transaction Register
    C. Revenue Exceptions Report
    D. Sales Journal by Customer

Question 147 of 150

All of the following are required steps during Oracle Receivables configuration except?

    A. Define Transaction Types
    B. Define Collectors
    C. Define Aging Buckets
    D. Define Approval Limits

Question 148 of 150

All of the following are collection report types in Receivables except?

    A. Billing and Receipt History
    B. Customer Credit Snapshot Report
    C. Transaction Register

D. Receipt Register

Question 149 of 150

Use the Approval Limits window to define
approval limits for?

    A. Adjustments:
    B. Credit Memo Requests
    C. Debit Memo Refunds (not its credit memo
        refunds)
    D. Receipt Write-Off

Question 150 of 150

All of the following are optional set up steps
during Oracle Receivables configuration except?

    A. Define Grouping Rules
    B. Define Transaction Sources
    C. Define Receivables Lookups
    D. Define Accounting Rules

ANSWERS

1) B - Yes, by assigning a deferred accounting rule to the Invoice.

2) C -Invoice Workbench

3) D- Receipt source

4) B- AR: Set Default Receipt Date

5) D - Transactions Workbench

6) A - Bill Receivables

7) A- Bill Receivables

8) A - AutoAccounting

9) B- The View Accounting Window

10) C- Commitments

11) A - Transaction Workbench

12) D - If AutoAccounting is based on sales credits.

13) C- RAM wizard

14) B- Invoice Rule

15) B- Split payment term functionality

16) B- Daily revenue rate, partial periods

17) Accounting Sets

18) Revenue Recognition Program

19) D- All of the above

20) B- False

21) B- FIFO

22) C- Deposit and Guarantees

23) A- Pending

24) D- All of the above

25) C- The date of your first copied invoice

26) C- Accounting rule

27) D- Concluded

28) D- Adjustments

29) B- Auto Invoice program

30) B – Its actually, When you credit a transaction, Receivables creates the appropriate accounting entries and credit any sales credit assigned to your salespeople

31) D- All of the above

32) A- True

33) D- Not closed

34) B- Exchange Rates

35) D- All of the above

36) D- Both A and B

37) A- True

38) B- Auto Invoice

39) B- Auto Invoice Import program

40) B- Indexes

41) B- Index Transaction Flexfield

42) A- Deposits and Guarantees

43) D- Deferred accounting rules

44) C- Oracle Costing

45) A- Revenue recognition execution report

46) B- Multiple Reporting Currencies

47) A- Pending

48) D- All of the above

49) A- Set the profile option AR: Use invoice accounting for credits profile option to No.

50) C- Auto Accounting

51) D- Function Security

52) D- All of the above

53) B- Record Sales credits

54) D- All of the above.

55) B- Cross Currency Exchange Gain/Loss report.

56) A- True

57) C- Application Rule Sets

58) Oracle Report Manager (ORM) or your customer can implement a program that understands the ORM protocol.

59) B- By using the Revenue Management Engine

60) D- All of the above

61) C- Auto Invoice validation program

62) Oracle Receivables automates this process with Payment-Based Revenue Management

63) A- Transaction Flex field

64) C- Invoice Transaction Flexfield

65) D- All of the above

66) D- All of the above

67) D- Applied Payment

68) A- Standard receipts and miscellaneous receipts.

69) B- Pending

70) C- Bill Later

71) C- Multiple copy

72) A- True

73) A- Guarantees and standard credit memos

74) A- Grace days

75) A- Cross currency receipts

76) D- All of the above

77) D- All of the above

78) A- Currency

79) C- Money orders

80) C- System Options window

81) D- All of the above.
82) A- Miscellaneous receipts

83) D- All of the above

84) C- Standard Reversal and Debit Memo Reversal

85) A- Automatic and manually entered receipts

86) A- Confirmed

87) C- Three

88) D- All of the above

89) B- Guaranteed

90) A- You can apply receipts to any type of transaction except guarantees and deposits.

91) B- If an invoice has one or more contingencies, then the Revenue Management Engine immediately defer revenue.

92) D- All of the above

93) B- Define Auto Accounting

94) A- AutoLockbox (or Lockbox)

95) D- All of the above

96) D- All of the above are true

97) D- All of the above are true

98) C- Interim tables

99) D – Its Clear Past Due Invoices Grouped by Payment Term and not post Past Due Invoices Grouped by Payment Term.

100)   B- Offset Discounts

101)   C- Both A and B

102)   B- Define AutoLock box

103)   D- All of the above are true

104)   D- No, its set the sequential
        document numbering profile option to
        'Always Used' or 'Partially Used and not
        Set the ACH Bank Account profile option
        to 'Always used' or 'Partially used.

105)   B- Customer's Address

106)   C- 5 Bucket Aging is not one of
        them, the 4th is Statement Aging.

107)   C- Prorate None

108)   A- Define Units of Measure

109)   C- Account Level

110)   C- Post: Post your receipts

111)   C- Standard and Factored

112)   E- All of the above are true

113)   C- Both A and B

114)   D- All of the above

115)   E- All of the above

116)   B- Its Automatic and not manually by creating a bills receivable batch using the Bills Receivable Transaction Batches window.

117)   C- All of the above

118)   B- Export

119)   C- Creation Stopped

120)   D- All of the above

121)   D- All of the above

122)   C- Bill Receivables Detail report

123)   D- Both A and B

124)   C- All of the above

125)   E- Both B and C

126)   C- Credit hold

127)   D- All of the above

128)   D- All of the above

129)   D- All of the above

130)   D- All of the above

131)   C- Both A and B

132)   C- Customer Address

133)   C- Receivables will not let you reopen previously closed accounting periods.

134)   D- Accounting Rule

135)   D- All of the above

136)		B- Commitments

137)		D- Does all of the above

138)		E- All of the above

139)		C- Its open Balances Listing and
not Balances Listing

140)		A- External and Internal

141)		B - Accounting Rules may be used
to recognize revenue across different
periods. Accounting Rules are redundant
as revenue will be recognized only when
payment is received; this is true in the case
of cash accounting.

142)		D- All of the above

143)		D- All of the above

144)   B- AutoCash rules

145)   D- All of the above

146)   B- Revenue Exceptions Report

147)   C- Define Aging Buckets

148)   C- Transaction Register

149)   C- It's actually Credit memo
refunds and not Debit memo refunds.

150)   B- Define Transaction Sources

www.ingramcontent.com/pod-product-compliance
Lightning Source LLC
Chambersburg PA
CBHW061019050326
40689CB00012B/2684